CIRCUS MAZES

Becky Radtke

DOVER PUBLICATIONS, INC.
New York

Bibliographical Note

Circus Mazes is a new work, first published by Dover Publications, Inc., in 1995.

International Standard Book Number: 0-486-28567-7

Manufactured in the United States of America
Dover Publications, Inc., 31 East 2nd Street, Mineola, N.Y. 11501

Note

Your attention, please! The circus is about to begin! Inside this book you will find 48 mazes featuring all of your favorite circus performers. They need your help to put on the circus! Read the verse at the bottom of each page and then help the acts put on a wondrous show.

Be sure to enter each maze where indicated with an arrow. After you've done the puzzles you can color each picture to complete your circus!

Solutions appear in the back of the book, beginning on page 53.

Before you stands the ringmaster
In the spotlight all alone;
He wants to welcome everyone
But needs his megaphone.

5

This little baby elephant
Has somehow gone astray;
She wants to find her mom and dad—
Please help her find the way.

6

Lead this pony to her trainer
And they will have it made—
For they have both been chosen
To lead the big parade.

7

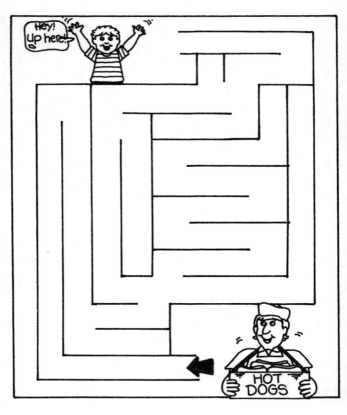

Charlie's getting hungry,
He'd like a bite to eat—
Lead this man up to him
So he can buy a treat.

Look at this circus tiger,
He's in a frantic state;
He's been looking everywhere
But cannot find his mate.

9

These pigs have formed a pyramid
But who will be on top?
Lead them to their sister
Or their act will be a flop.

10

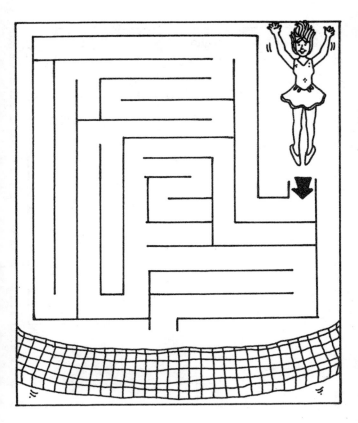

This lady's fallen from the tightrope
But look—she's not upset;
She knows you'll help her through the maze
Down to the safety net.

11

At the bottom of this maze
There is a tiny car;
It wants to find its passengers.
Do you see where they are?

This man has done the high dive—
Quick—help him on the double!
If he doesn't find the pool below
He'll really be in trouble.

13

This goofy-looking zebra
Will surely make you laugh—
But first help this funny fellow
To find his other half.

14

This mother hears her baby cry,
She's sure there's no mistake—
But she is undecided
On which path she should take.

15

At the top's a trapeze artist
Who goes by the name of Clancy;
He needs your help throughout the maze
16   To find his sister Nancy.

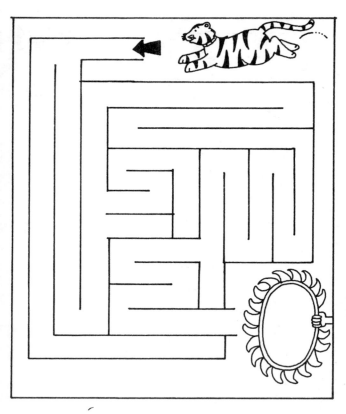

This tiger's busy practicing
To jump a little higher,
So when the hoop is finally lit
She'll jump right through the fire.   17

Before you is a little seal—
She's looking quite forlorn;
I'm sure she'd feel much better
If she could find her horn.

18

"The Magnificent Marching Majorettes"
Are the next act to go on;
Poor Margie cannot join them—
She's missing her baton.

19

This juggler threw three apples up
But they did not come down;
And now he needs your help before
They're eaten by a clown!

20

Next is an acrobatic act
But this team's incomplete—
Help this group up through the maze
To find their Cousin Pete.

Here are a pair of hippos—
They'd like to join the show;
They need to see the manager
But don't know where to go.

Silly Sue is fixing
To put on a funny face—
But however will she do this
Without her makeup case?

23

Sid needs to reach the stilts above
To be "The Tallest Man";
He's needed for the sideshow—
Please help him if you can.

24

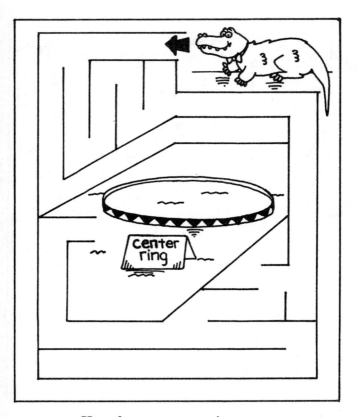

Here for your entertainment
Is a circus crocodile;
Show him to the center ring—
He'll thank you with a smile.

25

This is Polly Poodle
And she wants to do a trick—
Help her through the winding paths
So she can fetch the stick!

26

This is the circus seamstress—
She's feeling very sad;
She cannot draw up costumes
Without her sketching-pad.

27

Look at Leo Lion—
Listen to him roar!
He just finished a steak dinner
But apparently wants more!

This band member needs to signal
Intermission time has come;
But, alas, he cannot do this
Unless he has his drum.

This worker's in a panic—
It's her job to guard the ape;
But when she wasn't looking
He made a quick escape!

This tired little elephant
Has had a hectic day;
Won't you lead him to a place
Where he can hit the hay?

31

These horses seek their riders
But haven't got a clue—
Won't you lend a helping hand?
They don't know what to do.

The honey in the center
Is for this hungry bear!
Won't you kindly help her
Get from here to there?

Help Nicki and her friend up
To an elephant named Clyde;
For only fifty cents apiece
They both can have a ride.

Billy and his brother Joe
Both think it would be dandy
If you could lead them to the spot
Where they'll find cotton candy.

Mary Jean just noticed
That her balloons aren't there;
Quick—help her to retrieve them:
They're floating in mid-air.

Billy Bear wants his unicycle—
Can you please help him out?
He wants to jump up on its seat
And ride it all about.

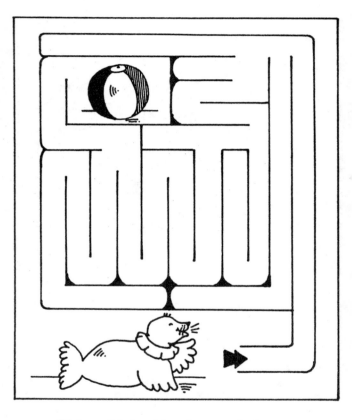

This seal is barking for your help—
Can't you hear him call?
Guide him through the winding paths
To find his striped beach ball.

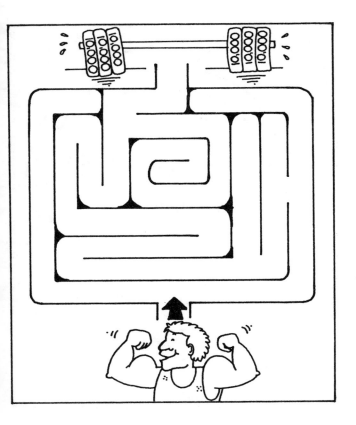

This very, very strong man
Puts on an act that's swell—
But before he can astound us
He'll need his huge barbell.

Goofy Gus is running fast,
He needs to catch that pig!
Lead him through the maze above
So he can get his wig!

Angie and Michelle were told
A toy-stand is quite near;
Won't you help them to it?
They want a souvenir.

41

Ryan would like some popcorn,
And he wants an ice cream bar—
We know that you can guide him
To where these goodies are.

These tigers are out and roaming free—
They know that something's wrong;
Lead them through the paths above
To where they both belong.

43

If you look at this page's top
You'll see a furry bunny;
He wants to hide inside the trunk—
44   He thinks it would be funny.

Marcus, the circus monkey,
Would appreciate it a bunch
If you would help him through the maze
So he could find his lunch!

45

Here's a baby monkey—
And he would be so glad
If you would lead him through this maze
So he can reach his dad.

"The Tremendous Mr. Tony"
Can do amazing things,
And he will gladly show you—
Just lead him to the rings.

This is Sherman Seal—
And if he gets his wish
He will quickly find his way
Up to the pail of fish.

Listen very carefully—
Do you hear a puppy's yelp?
The circus clown wants to find her,
But clearly needs your help.

49

Poor Mr. and Mrs. Leopard—
They have lost their tots!
Can you please help to find them?
They miss them lots and lots!

This tamer's lost his lion—
Which way should he go?
Could you please lead the way above?
He simply doesn't know.

"The Fearless Human Cannonball"
Is the act we've saved for last;
Thanks for coming to the show—
We hope you've had a blast!

Solutions

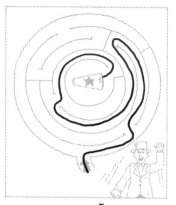

page 5

page 6

page 7

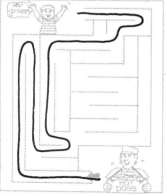

page 8

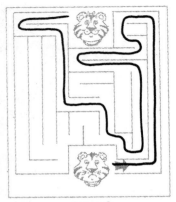

page 9

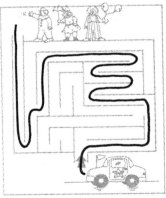

page 10

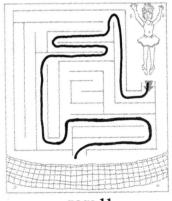

page 11

page 12

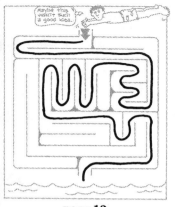

page 13

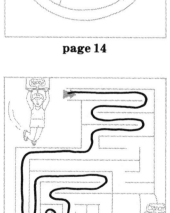

page 14

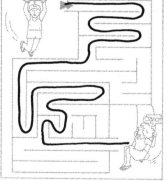

page 15

page 16

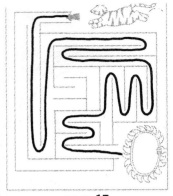

page 17

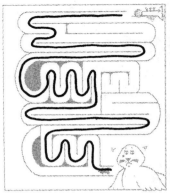

page 18

page 19

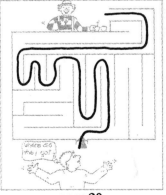

page 20

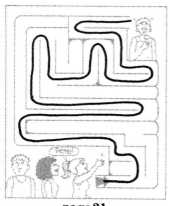

page 21

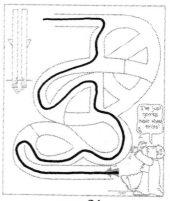

page 22

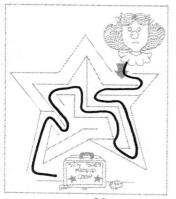

page 23

page 24

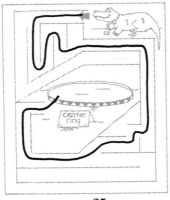

page 25

page 26

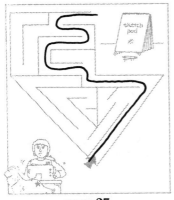

page 27

page 28

page 29

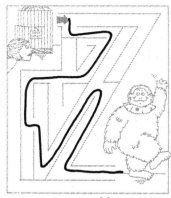

page 30

page 31

page 32

page 33

page 34

page 35

page 36

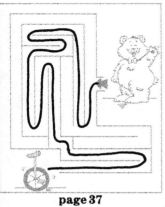

page 37

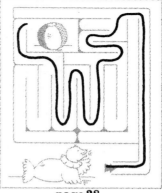

page 38

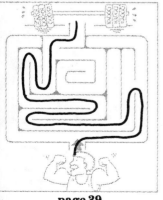

page 39

page 40

page 41

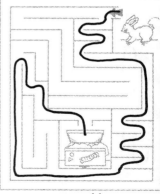

page 42

page 43

page 44

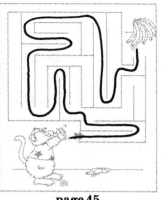

page 45

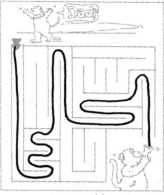

page 46

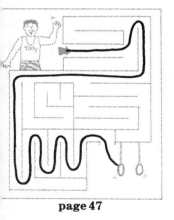

page 47

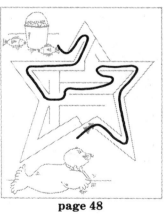

page 48

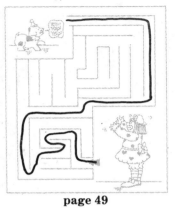

page 49

page 50

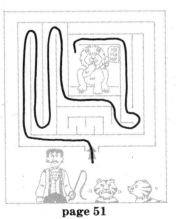

page 51

page 52